Six
STEPS TO
SIX FIGURES

ROCHELLE **Y. WILSON**

Dedication

I dedicate this book to my husband, Pastor Ishmael, and my children. My husband has pushed me over the years even when I didn't want to be pushed. He has coached and encouraged me through every transition of my life. Throughout the years, my husband has not only been moral support, but he has been inspirational support. His drive, tenacity and determination has prompted me to move and accomplish when I didn't feel confident. It also encouraged me to just do, even against all odds.

I also dedicate this book to my children who are so patient, flexible, and understanding. They never complain, even when I have to miss special moments. My children are my constant motivator. I have and continue to work so hard so that my children will have a quality of life that I didn't have. From the time I gave birth to my first child at the tender age of 15, I knew that I had to do whatever I could to make a better life for them. I also dedicate this book to every organization that allowed me to be an employee. I'm grateful for the skills and talents I've acquired. These skills will always be utilized with hopes of transforming the lives of others.

Lastly, I would like to thank my publisher Tressa Smallwood, CEO of Life Changing Books. Words cannot express my gratitude for all of your support and guidance. Your passion for authors is amazing. I appreciate your professionalism and drive which helped push me to complete this project.

Table of Contents

INTRODUCTION
How It All Started

I recall as a little girl growing up in the inner city the struggles that my family experienced on a continual basis. While my family hid our needs really well, it didn't negate the fact that we had a lot of tough times. The family concealed it so well that I didn't even know we lived in public/Section 8 housing until I was in college. I grew up with what I would call a pretty small family. It was small to me considering some of the family sizes today. In my household was my mother, grandmother, grandfather, 3 uncles and 1 great uncle. I was the only child my mother had and the only child in the house. This only child thing was tough because sometimes I felt like no one understood my perspective from the lens of a child. There was 8 of us in a 4-bedroom house with basement. My great uncle lived in the basement. That was his bedroom, which meant the basement could not be used for family time or special events.

There were many nights when we didn't have food but I can honestly say that I never went hungry and given my circumstances, that was good. I remember being a young child living in a house with drug dealers and different types of people from the streets. I never knew what I was going to see on a given day. Some of the things I was exposed to as a child, no child should be exposed to.

I could have seen a prostitute, pimp or pusher. In my home, there was always someone living with us who had a need. Gunshots in the neighborhood were the norm, and I quickly became numb to it. This was certainly not the environment to raise children or to grow a family. I started middle school wondering how I was going to make it. I mean really, I didn't know how I was going to make it. My mother didn't have a job and my household had a very limited income. There were only 2 individuals working in my home. The last time my mother was able to support me was when I was transitioning from sixth to seventh grade. After that, I was on my own. I was forced to take care of myself financially when I entered into middle school. My mother received little government assistance, so I had to make a way for myself. This adverse and humble beginning instilled qualities in me that I draw on now. The pain from my past pushed me – adding the fuel that I needed to accomplish a successful life. This became the starting point for the releasing of this book.

This book was written because I wanted to share all of my experiences that helped me to ascertain the level of success I have encountered thus far. My desire is to help shift more people from the remote thought of making six figures to getting them to that place. I want this book to inspire those who are trying to figure out how they can increase their financial portfolio, those who may feel like they keep hitting a brick wall with their business and career and finally those who simply want to make more money. My faith in God inspired me to work hard and pursue in a way that produced results.

Step 1

ESTABLISH GOALS

*THE POWER OF KNOWING WHAT YOU
WANT TO DO*

Six Steps to Six Figures

8

It is important to know what you want to do in life. Establishing goals will help you figure it all out. Not knowing what you want to do can cause you to waste valuable time, money, and resources. If you decide to go to college and you don't know what your major will be, take the first couple of semesters and outline how you want to use your degree. But, I recommend you declare a major as soon as possible. When you don't declare a major, you take generic classes that don't necessarily fit into any one major. This may cause you to waste money on classes that are not quite aligned with what you want to do because you don't know. You are given a certain time to declare a major. If you don't have goals set, you may end up selecting a major on the fly which could still not be a part of your long-term goals. I am not saying that in order to start college, you must be 100% sure of what you want to do. However, I am saying that the more you know about what you want to do, the less you may waste in time, money and resources.

As a little girl, I knew that I wanted to be a teacher. This didn't change once I got to high school. And when it was time for me to go to college, I knew exactly what I wanted to do. Knowing that I wanted to be a teacher guided me in all of my post-secondary decisions. I was able to make a sound decision about my program of study. This is not the case for some people. If you don't know what field you want to be in, then take some time to explore different areas and identify the one that most interest you. Goals become the blueprint for all of your dreams and vision. The purpose of setting goals is to have you think about what you want to achieve with the end in mind. You should establish a process that allows you to check your goals on a regular basis. Review goals monthly, bi-monthly, tri-monthly or every six months. It all depends on what you are trying to accomplish and how fast you are moving. You could be on a trajectory by which you get promotions every six months to a year, or you shift gears and try new things frequently. In this case, you may want to review goals often than not. If you stay in work areas longer than a year or two, then you can set short-term goals that align with the pacing of your movement. Your goals become a personal and internal accountability system for you. With this, you have to be transparent when setting goals because if you don't meet your expectations, then you have to accept the responsibility.

Falling short of your goals should not be the time to be hard on yourself or to beat yourself up; rather you should use this time to capture lessons learned. You can stand on the shoulders of your failures and receive the empowerment, encouragement, and momentum needed to continue to persevere and pursue your goals. Make every attempt to set realistic goals. They will help determine your pacing. It also helps you with being transparent regarding your capacity. Many people make the mistake of identifying goals that look good on paper and sound ambitious, but don't align with their capacity. Knowing your capacity is just as important as knowing your goals. Your capacity tells you how far you can and should go in any particular endeavor.

Here are four actions that will help with your goals:

1. Identify wins.

2. Monitor progress.

3. Pause at milestones and reflect.

4. Deal with stagnation expeditiously.

These acts will make it easy for you to identify the cause when you don't accomplish some of your goals. It's important to keep track of the barriers that can prevent you from making six figures plus. You don't want to continue to operate in error.

As mentioned previously, when you fail to reach goals, take the time to review your mistakes and use them as your "lessons learned." Don't stress out because you feel you are not "meeting the mark." Let the shortcomings serve as your motivation. During these times, you will get gentle reminders to let you know you are where you need to be. It could be as simple as getting a call back from a client or an opportunity to lead a project at work. You can't give up because giving up is not an option for someone who wants to make a six figure plus income. When you reflect on the milestones and all you have accomplished, it affords you with the opportunity to see your progress throughout the years. This also provides you with the space to reflect and celebrate the small or large milestones. You don't have to wait until something big happens in order for you to feel like you are making strides and accomplishing.

Setting goals is often a scary task for many. Many people run away from setting goals because of fear. For some, it is the fear of failure, and for others, it is the fear of "what if" or "what will they think." You know fear is tugging at you when you ask yourself, what will they think if this does not work? What if this all falls apart? These questions will haunt you and, if you are not strong, will prevent you from setting goals. Goal setting can also feel like the job of the "unknown." It is essential for you to embrace the idea that God has a plan for your life. This plan is made clear in Jeremiah.

Jeremiah 29:11 New International Version (NIV) 11 For I know the plans I have for you," declares the LORD, "plans to prosper you and not to harm you, plans to give you hope and a future.

And when you connect with God's will for your life, then you can start setting goals from a place of freedom and not fear. The benefits of establishing goals are paramount. Goals signify that you are clear and are sure of what you want. Goals are critical as they aid in various transitions and they guide your decisions around the types of jobs, experiences, and opportunities you pursue. This does not mean that there will not be times when you may have to take a job that doesn't quite align with your goals, but they keep you focused in the midst of misalignment or diversion. When you make a temporary detour, your goals are your roadmap that navigates you back on track. It is also helpful to create vision boards for goals to better help you to visualize them. And this ultimately becomes the plan needed to help you focus on your dreams.

Part of the goal-setting process involves determining whether you need formal education to enhance what you want to accomplish. Once a decision is made, you can move forward accordingly. There are certain work areas that reap more from formal education than others. For example, those who want to get into business may want to consider getting an MBA; while a telecommunications professional may need on-the-job training to excel rather than a formal degree. Formal education is not the answer for everyone, and there are very successful people who don't have formal degrees.

You have to do your research and due diligence to ensure you are making the best decision in your field. There are degrees that one could pursue in telecommunications, but the requisite skills could be acquired by working on the job over a period of time. The afore-mentioned are some best practices that can help with creating a successful portfolio. Maintaining a current portfolio or press kit, gives you an opportunity to showcase your work. It gives you the competitive edge. Maintaining a portfolio is a must and in some industries showcasing pictures is the best way to go. Potentials customers want to see visually what you can do and not just go by you telling them you can do it. Those in business need to retain sound best practices and business principles for business growth. And if these things are not embraced or learned, one could experience negative consequences. The negative consequences can cause you to miss opportunities, loose clients and subsequently money. Not to mention your professional and business representation will be at the center of it all.

"Goals become the blueprint for all of your dreams and vision."

Making the decision to pursue formal education with an identified major/concentration could give you a very solid head start. I remember when I was in undergraduate school, I entered as a freshman knowing that I wanted to be a teacher, and I knew that I didn't want to teach beyond the third grade. This identification put me in the early childhood education category. Early childhood education is birth to age 8.

Having this goal before college allowed me to select the major that best suited my needs. This gave me an advantage because I was able to seek out organizations while in college that were in my field of study. One of my college professors suggested that I get in my field of study before graduating. I did some research and found some great early childhood organizations. I was only able to take the advice from my professor because I had clear goals established. Otherwise, I could have been slightly confused and unclear about my starting point.

Getting into my field while in school meant I did non-payed work or, in layman's terms, volunteer work. Because I had declared early childhood education as my major, I was able to quickly seek out early childhood opportunities without delay. After calling and emailing many organizations about volunteering, I received a response from a very distinguished early childhood program that was recognized nationally and internationally. This organization not only said that I could volunteer, but they asked me if I wanted a permanent paying position. I remember speaking with someone from Human Resources, feeling like I was in a dream. It was an absolute win-win situation for me.

I was getting great experience from a premier organization and receiving compensation at the same time. What more could a college student and soon to be professional ask for? It all helped to position myself for bigger and better things. When I graduated as an undergrad, I already had one year of experience in my field. I'm grateful that my college professor encouraged me to get in my field as soon as possible. This one move afforded me the opportunity to get experience in my field of study while I was still in school. I had no idea that this one recommendation was going to be the thing that propelled my career in education, where I have remained faithful for 20 years. This was by far the best advice anyone could have ever given me to jumpstart my career. This one strategy helped me to position myself in the field of education. And I'm still reaping the benefits after learning so much.

Having goals is a great way to make sure you are positioning yourself for success, especially if you are in the right place at the right time. All throughout my career, and even as a businesswoman, I have always set goals. I always set long-term goals at the top of each year. Setting goals at the beginning of the year gives me a blueprint and makes me feel like I have some guidance and direction. I now look back at the times when I forgot to set my goals in January because I got so engrossed in the new year. By February and March, I was trying to figure out why things just didn't seem right or why I felt like I was lost. There's nothing worse than feeling lost. It is easy to say, "It is just February, I still have time." Then next thing you know, you look up, and it is August. You have lost most of the year.

16

I advise everyone to take the time to set goals at the beginning of the new year. If not, you may pay in a way that you hadn't envisioned. You can always tweak your goals and make adjustments throughout the year. You just need to have some direction. I can't emphasize the importance of carving out quiet time to write your goals. You need to meditate so you can get a clear head as you identify your goals. Dedicated time allows you to focus exclusively on what is important, which are your goals. One thing to remember while you are engaged in your goal-setting process is not to get caught up in what you see other people doing and feel compelled to duplicate them.

You have to completely focus on yourself, your goals, your dreams, your vision and your aspirations so that you are not distracted and run the risk of missing what you are assigned to do. It would be such a waste for you to do all of that planning, working and investing, and end up working towards something that was not for you. I know that it is tempting to duplicate what you see. You see nice websites, fliers, postcards, business cards things on television, and other promotional materials. The world doesn't need copycats; the world needs originals. You have to be your authentic self and that's why focusing on yourself is so important.

Once you are clear about doing what you should be doing and not worrying about others, you have to set realistic goals. Setting realistic goals will help you avoid unnecessary stress. I remember when I first started setting goals, I had some extremely ambitious goals. Those goals would have profited me and everyone around me, and would have made the world a better place. However, they were not realistic at all. In fact, those goals stressed me out so bad that I almost went into a state of depression. Because I am a hard worker and over achiever, I tried pushing myself to meet the goals, I went from being stressed to frustrated because I was unable to achieve the unrealistic goals. Being frustrated was the worst for me because I felt like a failure. The feeling of frustration can be quite intense. The toughest phase for me was the "blame phase." I blamed everyone I could, including myself. Blaming others shifted the focus off me and what I was doing or not doing, thus preventing me from achieving my goals. I didn't want to admit that the procrastination, lack of money/resources, fear or lack of wisdom was holding me back. It was so hard for me to face the failure monster that I had created. I just really wanted to see results. The torment of not getting results week after week, month after month and year after year was a lot to handle at times.

I finally got to the self-realization phase and identified barriers, what needed to be enhanced, and what changes I needed to make. I realized that sometimes looking in the mirror is not always going to make you feel good, but it will force you to take a good look at yourself and deal with your reality. And my reality was that I was not doing what it took to accomplish my six figure goals. My goal was to work hard to ensure that my children would have a better quality of life. At the rate I was going it felt like it was going to take a lifetime.

During this phase, it is important for you to be honest with yourself. Don't be afraid to be honest with yourself. If you can't be honest with yourself who can you be honest with? You owe yourself the truth so that you can be clear about your subsequent power moves. You will always have to operate with a high level of honesty. As you matriculate in your career or business, there will be times when you may not make the best decisions and honesty will be what you need, not excuses.

The level of honesty you engage in will determine the amount of success you experience when you try things again. You have to say it, acknowledge it and change. I suggest being as honest as possible because if not, you'll repeat the same mistakes again. You will get caught up in a vicious cycle. And the web can entangle you in a way that will make you want to give up. The plan is not for you to give up, but rather persevere and push toward your goals. If you are honest with yourself, the stress connected to failing can be overwhelming.

When you have big, impactful dreams, there will always be a level of stress. However, when you are clear about what you should do, it will surely minimize your stress levels. Again, the focus should be on you and not what others are doing. While it can be helpful to glean from people who are successful or even get a mentor, it is important to know without a shadow of a doubt what you should be doing. Just because your friends are doing something, does not mean you should be doing that "something" too. What your friends are doing is for them. Your friends' plot is not your plot, and your plot is not theirs. Your goals aren't your mother's or your father's. We are all individuals, and we should work towards our own goals. I know some people will try to influence you by making suggestions about what you should do. You can certainly take their advice into consideration. But at the end of the day, make sure you set goals that are for you and only you.

People often are afraid to set goals for future success because they worry about looking too aggressive or they are concerned about people who want to do what they are doing but are afraid to move. Some people are naturally aggressive and assertive, and these are characteristics for those I call "goal diggers." This means your goals allow you to aggressively search for what you want. Your goals help you establish your "end in mind." The end in mind is the place where you ultimately want to be. This should be your dream; what you want to end your life doing. For some of us, being aggressive and assertive is not part of our nature. We have to put a little effort in it. That's me! During the early years of my career and as an entrepreneur, I was very passive and soft spoken. I would let people take advantage of me. I wouldn't speak up, and I would let opportunities walk right by me. I always thought that my work would speak for me. One day my mindset around that changed. It changed when I noticed people getting promotions, recognition, increases, and opportunities who didn't work as hard as I did. These individuals didn't produce great results like I did nor did they have my expertise or credentials. What I noticed about these individuals was that they had a voice and made sure everyone around them knew it. They advocated for themselves. The people that I am talking about didn't let others bully them or run over them.

Self-advocacy proved to work for them and yielded great re-sults. These were individuals that were intentional about making sure key stakeholders knew who they were. In my mind, I called that "schmoozing" and in their mind, it was "letting them see me." This really hit home one day when I was having a candid conversation with my boss' boss. This was not any boss' boss; she was the chief operating officer and someone whom I respected greatly. She was giving me positive feedback about a project that I was managing and complimented me on my work ethic. In fact, she just didn't compliment it, she gave it a commendation. She noted that my work ethic was "impeccable."

To have someone say that my work ethic was impeccable in my eyes was like receiving an award. I say this because the longevity that I have had in my career is attributed to a strong work ethic. This work ethic carried over into my business practices as an entrepreneur. I was on cloud nine about her praise, and then it hit me, I still hadn't received a promotion or increase even with an impeccable work ethic. All I could say was "wow." How could an impeccable work ethic not yield some type of reward in return? It was then that I realized that I was missing something.

As we continued to talk, I asked my boss' boss about my future in the organization and for some sound professional advice. This was a huge step for me because I didn't want to look desperate. You have to know when to ask for help and when to seek out wisdom. You should get wisdom from someone above your level. If you do not get wisdom, you are bound to stay at your current level with no momentum and no traction. There is one thing that she noted that resonated with me. She said, "I never see you on the top floor." Now, you must know that the top floor was where all of the senior executives worked. She said you have to let the CEO and COO see your face more. And instantly, I thought "*I am not a schmoozer.*" But when I called to mind those who were promoted and recognized, they exhibited some characteristics that I frowned upon.

These people made sure they were seen on the top floor often. That's when I had another aha movement. You have to let people put a face to your work product. I also discovered that when you make your face known, you are given opportunities to share about yourself and your work based on your perspective, not your bosses'. A lot of times we wait and expect our bosses to promote us, our work and our capabilities. I have learned over the years that this doesn't always happen, especially if your boss doesn't like you or is intimidated by you or wants to get the credit for something you have done. My advice to eradicate this problem is to make sure you have an alternate person of influence, other than your boss, who knows your character, capacity, and work ethic. This small nugget can open up doors and get you out of tight situations.

After about a year of watching this play out, I knew I needed to change. My problem was I never wanted to look like I didn't respect authority or that I wasn't a team player. What I eventually learned was that you can have a voice AND respect authority; you can have a voice AND be a team player. So I decided to change my behavior and began to speak up. And for those who are naturally aggressive and assertive, I say speak up, show out and position yourself. Part of positioning yourself includes finding your niche. Your niche deeply connects you to what you are doing. Some areas are broad because there are many layers. As you begin to pull back the layers, then you can decide which direction you are going in. You can be confident even if someone wants to do the same thing that you are doing.

Focus on your niche and let everything else work out on its own. There are times where you may decide to focus on one area within your field. In this case, your focus is getting all of the necessary training, credentials, and skills that you can to position yourself in ways that have a positive impact on your growth opportunities. The key is working to position you with skills, abilities, and/or education. This also makes you marketable. This also puts you in a place that I call the "competitive advantage". You will have the advantage because you are well equipped.

If you are in a room with five people competing for the same position, what is going to distinguish you? Why would the employer select you? It will be the aligned acquired skills and education that you have obtained. Education is also important when talking about setting goals. We live in a society where we see lots of great things happening in the lives of people. We see those who are wealthy, those with successful businesses and careers. Some of these individuals have experienced these great results without having a college degree and to those in this awesome category, I say "bravo," "wonderful" and "well deserved."

While these stories are amazing and should be encouraging and inspiring, we need to be careful in thinking this will be the outcome for everyone. Although this type of scenario exists all over the world, across races and creed, there is still a major role that education plays relative to our advancement. We have to be careful not to give the impression that we devalue education as a society. For some communities, education was the key that unlocked some doors and provided a way of escape out of some pretty challenging situations. Education is a powerful tool and resource. Personally, education has been a powerful instrument. As a former teen mom and high school drop-out, education created a window of opportunity for me. Education literally saved my life. I had a baby when I was 15, and during that time my mother was a substance abuser, so you can only imagine what I was dealing with. No child should have to go through these kinds of tough times.

My mother was receiving government assistance, and I had no idea what life was going to be like for me or my baby. All I knew was that I had this little human being who was depending entirely on me. His father did not provide for him physically, spiritually, emotionally, financially…did I say financially? It wasn't until I decided to go back to high school after dropping out that I had an "aha" moment about education. I had the baby in January and thought that I shouldn't return to school because I would be too far behind. I decided to do my own thing, but this didn't last long. I thought to myself if I don't go to school, then I won't have much knowledge. And I wanted to be knowledgeable and smart. I didn't know how I had gotten to the place of dropping out of school, especially because I was a child who loved school and knew that I wanted to be a teacher since the sixth grade. You couldn't pay me to miss a day when I was in elementary school. I remember wanting to go to school, even when I was sick. I am so glad I changed my mindset and saw the value of education. Not only did I go back to high school, but I also went to college and, subsequently, graduate school. My education shifted my professional trajectory and helped my career greatly. Education is one resource that crosses all borders as well as socio-economic statuses. Here I was the salutatorian in elementary school, who was getting ready to get off course and minimize my potential. Going back to school to get my education was one of the best decisions I ever made. I can't believe that I was going to throw my future out of the window by deciding to not receive a sound education.

In many states it's hard to get a decent job without a college education. Let's not even talk about a high school education. Therefore, we have to continue to push for education and keep it a viable option for all generations. It is never too late to get an education. We live in a day where the unemployment rate is not quickly decreasing, and many people are not hopeful about our economic system. There are people competing for jobs in fast-food chains, making minimum wage. In different industries, men and women with advanced degrees are competing for entry-level positions. There is not an adequate supply of jobs. As a result, we have people with PhDs who are competing for mid-level managerial positions. I have witnessed this over the last eight years. There was a time when I was a manager trying to fill vacancies and I would have a reasonable amount of resumes that matched the posted jobs. Slowly over the years, it moved from a reasonable amount of resumes to close to 100 resumes for a non-managerial position. Lots of people with advanced degrees were submitting their resumes. I remember reviewing some resumes for an entry-level specialist position, and I was astonished by a resume I had received. The candidate was more than just over-qualified. Baffled as to why the candidate had submitted the resume, I decided to call. I got the candidate on the phone, introduced myself and begin to address the nature of my call.

There was one important thing I wanted the candidate to know, which I knew would change the interest level. What I had to share is typically the deal breaker in every employment transaction at the recruitment and hiring phases. I had to tell that candidate that the salary was more than likely $30K to $50K less than his current salary requirements. It was clear that the candidate would have to take a pay cut in the position. Once I shared the news, the candidate still wanted to move forward because there were not a lot of job opportunities in the area that candidate was trying to get into. He clearly had some goals that were driving his decisions.

Your goals will help you position yourself. They will speak to where you go or shouldn't go. Your goals should ultimately align with the vision you have set for yourself. Everyone should have a personal vision and mission statement that is tied to your goals. What is the end in mind for you? What do you ultimately want to do? When you identify that, then all you do should be centered on that. Everyone needs this kind of roadmap.

When I created my vision and mission statement for myself, it helped me get laser focused about the things that I should do. It became easy to say "no" to things that didn't align with my vision and mission statement. I knew that I wanted a six figure salary which was going to require lots of hard work. I was not going to invest countless hours in working on various databases and attending technology conferences if I wanted to be an internationally known business expert traveling and speaking all over the country. I needed to invest in those activities that aligned to my vision.

When you align to your vision, you are also able to acquire the right skillset over time. When you are in the vision space, you don't find yourself wasting time, not even an hour. The right skill-set will put you on the road to increase financially. There are so many people with degrees that they don't use them. Perhaps having a personal vision and mission statement could have helped them save money spent on college and aided in the proper redirection. When the right skills, experience, and education are lined up it makes it easier for you to get a promotion, increased business and extended opportunities.

Understanding your talents are so critical. When you know your talents, then you are able to stand on the shoulders of what you can do well. Having a sound understanding of your talents can help launch you into a completely different category that will ultimately increase your earning potential. You can build on your talents by having a part-time job or consulting gig. If you sell services and goods, this is a great way to help supplement your income. As you advance in business and or your career, you will have to continually assess your talents and look for ways to increase your revenue. Even if your talent is not your passion, maximize it so you can build your earning potential.

All that has been shared thus far is to help you to be successful and to get you closer to that six figure income. Let me be honest, success is not promised or guaranteed. And no, you just don't wake up successful. But with some hard work and faith, you can get real close to success. In order for you to maximize your earning potential and cross over to six figures, even if you are not currently making six figures, you are going have to work hard. It is that simple. I know hard work was mentioned before. I just really wanted to stress a sense of urgency around hard work. Success doesn't come easy and oftentimes will not lay out a bed of roses for you. If you study most successful people and how they made it, they will have many stories about what their success cost them – lost sleep, many tears, long hours, etc. They will likely tell you that they gave and didn't get back; "HEARD NO" but kept on pushing. All of this happened before they got a breakthrough, a big door opened, or they got their big break.

Another critical element when establishing goals is branding. Branding is important when it comes to positioning. You are your own brand whether you are working for yourself or for someone else. Branding forces you to ask yourself what is driving people to you, your business product, or service. Branding is essentially your promise to the public. What are people getting when they experience you? What can people count on getting from you consistently when they encounter or interface with you. That would be your brand. When setting your goals consistency adds value to your brand. Over promising and under delivering can destroy your brand. Things like colors, experiences, and symbols are the visual things that people are drawn to. This is what branding is all about. If you can afford it, hire a person or company that specializes in branding because it can make or break you. It is wise to focus on one or two things you do really well rather than trying to do a lot of things. It's the same if you are providing a service, make sure you have perfected your service and or goods. The public will appreciate quality over quantity. This is when you have to deliver on what you communicated you would. Don't contaminate your brand by over promising. You want to deliver and do that consistently so that the public knows that you are reliable.

"Branding is essential to your advancement."

Having a solid personal brand is also important for you as an individual and an entrepreneur. What you do and how you do it spills over into your business or career. If you are not consistent personally, you will more than likely not be consistent in business or in your career. If you never keep your word, this will surely transition to your business. It is important to gauge your personal brand like you would the brand for your business. Protecting your brand is something that every business owner and professional needs to be mindful of.

Make sure that the people that are representing your brand, do so in the manner in which you would present it. It is your job to make sure the people around you understand your brand completely and maintain its integrity. It is very easy for people to misrepresent your brand out of ignorance. Whenever I am coaching a client, I always suggest that every person that represents them should go thru extensive training on understanding your brand. This is very important when others have to communicate your brand in your absence.

Another critical element in branding is making sure what you are giving to the public is a true reflection of what you want public to receive. You can burn your brand by simply sending the wrong message to key players and influencers. On the other hand, you can grow your brand and expand because people are selling you like a showroom car. This is the purest form of networking that there is. Networking is a way to expand and promote your brand.

As a professional or entrepreneur, it's always good to engage in reflective practice. This means that you are ever reflecting, evaluating and making necessary changes based on your evaluation. I remember taking some time to reflect on my career as an educator. This was a time when I reflected on the various roles I had as a teacher, early childhood coordinator, reading specialist, and administrator. It dawned on me that I had not branded myself as it relates to establishing a niche or an expert area.

As I vetted my resume, it was apparent that I had more experience in early childhood education. I took that information and began shifting my focus and presentation of my skillset. I had now started the process of promoting myself as an early childhood expert. People are more prompted to receive and acknowledge experts over those who are a novice in their field. I knew that eventually I wanted to do some consulting work. This was the perfect time to start getting my hands dirty in the world of consulting.

If you desire to become a consultant in any field – from fashion to education to administration you have to get some level of expertise. Typically, when people serve in the role of consultant, they are in a position of advising and giving support in a particular area that they have experience in.

What is an expert?

1.Rochelle's definition of an expert is: one who has a solid content understanding of a particular body of work that is backed and substantiated by a reasonable amount of experience and education that is directly aligned.

2.Webster's definition of an expert: A person who has a comprehensive and authoritative knowledge of or skill in a particular area.

After I decided to get on the expert track, I developed a detailed plan with goals that served as my roadmap. About a year later, I received my first official offer as an early childhood expert consultant. I accepted a consultation job for a well-known education agency, which started off paying $100.00 per hour. I could not believe it! I had been consulting many years prior to this contract, however I was not getting anything close to $100 per hour. I was ecstatic! I could not believe that I had a contract that was going to yield over a quarter of a million dollars. My first consulting assignment paid me $30 per hour. At the time I was excited about this amount as I was just starting out. I can't stress enough the importance of developing some level of expertise in a specific area. It definitely adds value to your portfolio. It also puts you at the top of the list in comparison to other people. It will also put you in a very different compensation category. One that will feel like an upgrade.

When companies and organizations are looking for support in certain areas, they look for people who have the right background. They are not interested in people who think they can, but people who know they can and have proven that they can. And lastly, being an expert will quickly put you on the road to making six figures. The education agency contract allowed me to earn in six months more than I had made in one year with my regular 9 to 5 job, where I was getting paid a little shy of $90K. Again, I was in mere amazement that someone thought my expertise was worth what they were paying me. You must have and maintain a certain level of expertise that will keep you in the game, and ultimately, keep you in demand.

Becoming an expert affords you the opportunity to serve as a consultant at an advanced level. The large agency contract was a big accomplishment for me, and it not only allowed me to position myself professionally but also financially. Consulting can be very lucrative and profitable if you leverage your skillset. If you are looking for another income stream and a quick way to hit the six-figure mark, then you need to identify two or three areas of consultation. I don't want you to miss this key component of expanding your financial portfolio. Consulting is very flexible and something that you could do along with a full-time job. You could consult in the evenings, early mornings, remotely or even on the weekends. This was another aha moment for me. Here I was trying to get a promotion on my job and looking for jobs that paid more. And my increase was right in my hand; it was part of the repertoire of skills I had. What I grossed on a part-time basis with the agency consulting contract was more than the yearly salary of a senior-level employee. This is a sure way to increase your earning substantially.

Having education goals can be a valuable tool or resource when trying to navigate thru life. Depending on the career, trade or industry you choose, formal education may be a driving factor/force in your overall success. A postgraduate education is becoming more of a pre-requisite for success in some areas. There are industries that require you to have a Bachelor's degree and/or Master's as well as a PhD. Let me be honest and transparent: Education does not guarantee success. In some industries, a college degree is not required or necessary. For fields such as IT and construction, having the proper certifications can be more productive and align with the nature of that industry. There are people who are making six figures without a degree, but they have studied their craft and have become certifiable experts in their field. If you are in a field where certifications are acceptable, then you need strategies of acquiring these certifications that align with your ultimate salary goals. Educating yourself is key when you are trying to increase in any field.

What I've found to be true is education can serve as a solid launching pad for anyone. It adds value to what you are trying to accomplish. A word to the wise: try to get your degree in the area that you are sure you want to be in. Having what I call "sure" goals will help you determine the best major for you. They will help steer you, so that you don't get a business degree if you really want to become an astronaut. This kind of unintentional planning will cause you to waste time and money. I can't stress enough the need to be intentional about getting an advanced education that will allow to you smoothly move along in your career or business. This will save you trouble in the long run. Some parts of our society have a difference of opinion regarding the value of education. I am not going to get in the middle of that debate. However, I must note that getting an education whether from an institution of higher learning or by professional development will add value to anyone's career and or business.

Now, it is possible to position yourself without having a college degree. This can be done with one key element: HARD WORK.

You have to do things slightly different than those who decided to go the college route. The first one is taking on extra assignments at work. If you are already working, then seek out opportunities on your job that would let you gain diverse experiences. These duties will give you exposure in various offices. With each assignment, you will learn something different and build your resume. The goal is to diversify your skillset and expand your portfolio. You will also gain experience in areas and industries that you otherwise would not be exposed to.

Secondly, you can combine traditional job experiences with a business venture. I have been a licensed real estate agent for well over a decade. As a dual-career agent, I was able to earn extra money working in real estate as well as earn a salary that comes from my full-time position as an educator. These two streams only helped to sustain my six figure income. As you could imagine, working in both areas allowed me to increase my earning potential, which aligned with my goals and positioned me for advancement. You too can get closer to six figures and position yourself for increase by combining a full-time position with a business venture that allows you to work on a part-time basis. It's all about leveraging your skills and strengths.

Thirdly, you can position yourself by using any special talents. If you are a singer, you could consider singing part-time to supplement your full-time job. Once you build your capacity and get your name out in the public, then you can begin to take multiple engagements, which will help you brand yourself. After you build your client base, then you can explore the options of working your talents full-time. If the demand is there, then you must seize it. In order to maximize this, you will need long term goals, a strategy and wisdom. As you expand in your career or business, it may also help to get a coach or a mentor. This is someone who can guide you based on their experiences. The benefits that you get from a coach or mentor, outweighs any investment you have to make.

Over time all of this hard work, combined with meeting your goals could position you for jobs that require degrees because your diverse experiences now can be equated to having a graduate degree. Those extra assignments in the workplace can provide you the insights into what other offices are doing, so you can begin to strategically align and position yourself with the department that best suits your goals.

Everything you do must be paired with hard work and a strong work ethic. Having a sound work ethic is paramount and instrumental in the positioning process. It doesn't matter if you are in your ideal job/position, having a sound work ethic is a test you will have to take. Also, let's not forget how important character is. No matter how much you goal set you need strong character in order to succeed in your career or business. Your employer and your customers need to know if they can count on you. Can you be trusted? Do you deliver on your promises? People will remember those great qualities when they are considering hiring you, promoting or patronizing your business. When you have goals for advancement in all areas of your life, you must be mindful of the importance of a sound work ethic. This is essentially your work and business character. Good character is something that will give you longevity. It involves things like integrity, honesty, trustworthiness, consistency, dependability, and being a team player. These characteristics will cause people to connect with you because they know you add value.

Now, let's discuss something that is critical to your growth as you work to matriculate to the six figure income bracket and that is organization. Organization is an essential ingredient for your short and long term goals. If you expect to excel in your career or business, the first thing you must understand and embrace is the importance of putting things together in an orderly and functional manner. Being organized means having systems in place that will help you manage your workload in a structured way. It allows you to completely manage all of your services, goods and offerings adequately. These are questions you want to answer to help you identify your organization capacity.

Do you have the ability to manage multiple tasks and

assignments? How do you remember the meetings you have from day to day? What is your response turn-around time? Do you have a process for tracking inventory? Do you know how much money you bring in monthly?

It's not about having a cute journal or a nice notebook. While women typically love cute journals and I do to, it so much more than that. It is all about organization. Experiencing any level of success will have more to do with organization than anything else. When you are not organized, you miss appointments, forget to respond to people, you don't track your work, and subsequently you will lose money and opportunities.

Do you know all of the appointments you have for a given week or do you remember a meeting five minutes beforehand because you saw the Post-it on your desk? You need systems to help you balance the demands of life. What if ten clients need you to provide a particular service in one day, how will you manage that? Will you keep it in your head and do you have a system for writing things down to plot out your day? It is not OK for you to forget a meeting or a request from a client or your supervisor. After so many times of forgetting, consumers and employers will not trust you, especially if you fail to execute or carry out a major deliverable. This behavior will have a chilling effect at your workplace and your business.

You should adopt or create an organizational system that

works for you. For some, writing a daily to-do list is effective; others may need a monthly or weekly calendar. Whatever you choose, use a system that best fits your style because if you don't, you will be frustrated by your inability to manage the affairs of your business or career. If you are managing multiple streams of income, this is going to be essential.

Now, let's look at the benefits of relationships. Making and leveraging good relationships is another critical element as you strive to position yourself for greatness. You may not get the promotion in the department that you work in, but you could very well get it from another department or office because of relationships you have. It is always wise to try to network with people from different offices and industries because for every person that will say no, there will be one willing to say yes someplace else. Connecting outside of your scope of work and/or industries may present you with options that you didn't know about. It also puts you on the top of the list when opportunities arise. This is a form of networking and can greatly benefit you.

You may find yourself connecting with a manager who is not popular but that connection could still open a major door for you. There was a manager I had and some people didn't like him because they didn't understand him. I felt like I was assigned to him because I was the last to be hired on the team. This person turned out to be extremely generous and offered me a promotion that positioned me in ways that I could have only dreamed of. In business, networking with people in and out of your industry can be very profitable. Over the years, I have received speaking engagements and consulting opportunities just by networking or by selling products to different people. These are people who I didn't previously know and was able to connect with because I decided to network. You have to be intentional about networking. It is not just about being social, but it is about having an end in mind.

Many years ago, I was not very social. I am an introvert by nature and I had to force myself to be consistently social. It became easier over time especially when I started to experience the benefits of being social and networking. I am not saying act fake and phony, but what I am saying is know why you are doing what you are doing. If you don't, you will just be doing lots of networking, lots of giving hugs and taking selfies, without any contact information or leads that will help grow your business or accelerate your career.

SIX STEPS TO SIX FIGURES
Planner

What are your next steps?

_____

_____

_____

List any barriers

_____

_____

_____

What resources do you need?

_____

_____

_____

Completion Date

_____

_____

_____

WOW!!!
WORDS OF WISDOM

Integrity

Integrity is one of the keys to success and the medicine for a good life. Integrity will give you the longevity you'll need for where you're going.

Reflections

Reflections

_____

_____

_____

_____

_____

_____

_____

_____

_____

_____

_____

_____

_____

_____

_____

_____

_____

_____

_____

_____

Reflections

Reflections

_____

_____

_____

_____

_____

_____

_____

_____

_____

_____

_____

_____

_____

_____

_____

_____

_____

_____

_____

_____

_____

Step 2

POSITION YOURSELF

GET IN THE DOOR

Six Steps to Six Figures

You may have heard of the saying "Just get your feet in the door." I never understood this phrase until I had a first-hand experience with what it really meant. This quote primarily refers to getting in on a low level at an organization or company job. These opportunities should not be overlooked because they can be used to display your other skills to the organization and they can give business owners the opportunity to turn one-time customer into a consistent client. When an individual is willing to take an opportunity or position that may be beneath their current skillset or at a low compensation level. In some instances, the opportunity, project or position may not involve compensation. Most successful people will tell you how they started out and it is usually because they got their feet in the door. There are millionaires who started their careers or businesses by working in the mail room or selling lemonade at a stand.

For those people, the mail room served as a way to get their feet in the door. You can't be afraid to start low. Don't get upset because you are not getting paid for what you are doing right now.

This is the time where you need to take advantage of the experience, build your resume or portfolio, and wait to be shifted to your next level. I too have my own story about how I benefited from getting my feet in the door. At one point in my career, I knew that it was time for me to transition. I had been looking for a job for about a year and was only called three times for an interview. I remember feeling so discouraged because I had literally applied for 100-plus jobs and only got three calls. I was applying for jobs that I knew I was qualified for, but yet, no company seemed interested. One day, I received a call from an organization that I was interested in, and boy, was I excited! Finally, someone called me back!

This had the potential to damage my confidence and almost did. I had to continue to give myself pep talks. At the time, so many people were interested in working for this organization and the available positions were limited. As I searched through various job banks, I noticed that there were some good opportunities that would allow me to get my feet in the door. I got so tired of not getting any calls that I ended up applying for a position that was not at my current compensation level. At that moment it didn't matter because it was time for me to leave. I was determined to make something happen. I had enough of working hard with no recognition, reward or promotion. Please don't get me wrong; I was grateful for my job at the time, especially having survived cuts and reductions in force. I had never been fired and I was proud of that. None of this, however, trumped my desire to move on to something bigger and better. So for this new opportunity, the hiring manager called me for an interview three days after I had submitted my application. I interviewed and was hired for the job. During this interview, I used my updated portfolio with exemplars of work that I had done as well as data connected to my previous work performance.

Three months after I was hired, I received a detail or temp assignment in another department within that organization. Initially, I pushed back because I viewed it as something negative but it turned out to be a beneficial move. I was given a huge project while on detail and because of the nature of the work, I was in direct contact with senior management. The face time that I had with senior leaders was unbelievable. Really! I was shaking my head with the amount of contact that I had on a daily basis with the senior executives. Two months after the detail, I applied for another job within my office that paid more money and I was granted the promotion. This position launched me into a higher income bracket.

Finally, I was tapping into the goal I had set for myself – making six figures. I had known professionals and business owners who were making well over six figures and in some instances, seven figures. While I wanted to make six figures, it felt like it was far-fetched considering my background. However, I made a personal commitment to work hard and take advantage of every learning opportunity to get me to six figures and I was willing to put in the work. You too will have to be willing put in the work in order to get to six figures.

Remember, it is critical that you don't allow yourself to get upset because you are not receiving compensation for a particular job you are doing. Your focus has to be on getting the experience that will help you grow to the next level. Once you get the experience, put any new skills, tasks or additional responsibilities on your resume to assist with future growth. Just be patient and you'll see the financial increase come in time. You have to have this mindset as you push forward. I've held many positions over the past 20 years in which I did things and were given additional responsibilities that did not come with more money.

As an entrepreneur, you may have to render some free services to get your feet in the door of organizations, to get new clients, or even to get exposure. When I was an image consultant once upon a time, one of the things I did was style people at no charge so that I could get my name out in the community. Ultimately I got more clients. Whatever your business, consider providing free demonstrations at special events or local community-sponsored activities to build a clientele. The question you must ask yourself as a professional and as an entrepreneur: Are you willing to do whatever it takes to get in that door? After you have done your research, weighed the cost and reviewed all the pros and cons, are you willing to take that big step, that leap of faith, that forward lunge to your next level of greatness, increase and ultimate profitability? The key to succeeding is knowing that when you get in that door, it is then your time to shine. So, have confidence in yourself. So that when its time to shine you can authentically show your true worth. And that is what I did after getting in and moving on. My portfolio increased and I was given a great platform. What has been evident in my journey is that everyone just needs an opportunity. The only thing between you and your counterparts is an opportunity. You can be just as talented as the next professional or provide great services and/or goods like the next business owner, however it will ultimately be an opportunity that will set you apart.

One day during an aha moment, it occurred to me, I was conducting a staff training that my direct supervisor was getting paid to do. I really had a hard time understanding why if we were doing the same work, then why weren't we all getting paid for it. I asked questions of senior managers and could never get specific answers. After years of seeing this, I went through a phase of being angry and wanting to rebel. Yes! I wanted to rebel! I wanted to speak directly to what appeared to be an equity issue.

I had a quick reality check after I discovered that my rebellion was not going to change anything. One of the key parts to making sure you are doing what needs to be done at the right time is getting the right counsel and wisdom. It is really easy to rush and make a decision out of anger and frustration. You always have to be sure your temporary decisions don't have a permanent effect on your career or business. This was definitely a constant lesson for me as situations repeated themselves. I kept getting all of these additional responsibilities without additional compensation. There were many days when I wanted to lash out and tell everyone what was on my mind, how frustrated I was and how unfair things were. These are the times where my mentor would call or email me some wisdom that I needed for the moment. My husband had a way of keeping me calm and rational. I got tired of working hard while feeling so much frustration and anger. I was filled with these two emotions almost every day. The feeling of being overworked and underpaid had taken its toll.

Then there was another aha moment. This aha moment was connected to the importance of documentation. This prompted me to start an aggressive documentation process and subsequent norm for myself. I started documenting my additional duties, especially the heavy hitters. These were job responsibilities that looked really good on resumes. My philosophy was that since I had done the work and was successful, then I had a right to put it on my resume.

What did I learn from all of this? What one company won't pay you for, another company will. It is all about timing and finding the right job. I started treating the additional tasks and duties as free professional development. I essentially saw it as the company I was working for giving me free services and free training. This thought helped me to get through when I didn't feel valued. Once I got through this, then I knew it was time to transition.

Knowing when to transition when you have been over-looked has to be strategic. You don't want to make an irrational de-cision that will hurt you later. Even if you are absolutely right in your reasoning for leaving, you still need to be strategic. You must consider the potential impact at every level. Depending on your role and what you do, there could be a political impact. If you are influential in the community, there could be a community impact. Lastly, if you don't have a financial plan, there could be a serious financial impact. During tough or delicate transitions, you must be careful with your words and try to remain calm. You don't want to badmouth your superiors or others, and then get caught in a web of gossip and inappropriate sharing of information, all because you were emotional. I remember when I had to make the decision to transition from one position to the next. It wasn't because I was not getting a good salary, although I surely wanted more compensa-tion. I felt extremely mishandled and disappointed. I didn't leave for reasons like a hostile work environment or because of a verbally abusive boss. I left because I was tired of competing against myself.

After two years of excelling and experiencing good gains on a project, no one seemed moved by it. No one cared that I had produced major work that impacted lots of students, schools and families. The one time I felt acknowledgement was when my boss' boss thanked me for doing a great job. We were in the bathroom and she walked in with me. She greeted me and then thanked me for leading the efforts for a big initiative. This thank you would have been great if we were in our office, in a meeting, or around some of my other colleagues, but this was done in the bathroom. I can recall sharing this story with a friend, who said, "Don't give me a bathroom thank you, give me a public thank you." It was really not about getting a bathroom thank you, but it was about the need for me to have my senior leaders recognize me for my efforts in a more intentional way and that just did not happen.

One thing I will note here is that this particular scenario sheds light on the need for organizational and office culture to celebrate and acknowledge the accomplishments and efforts of its team members. This is critical at every level, whether you are a small business with a team of four or a Fortune 500 company. A culture of appreciation will breed consistent practices, motivate staff to perform, eliminate equity issues and decrease ambiguity when it comes to office norms and practices. I work and perform the way that I do because of sound work ethic. However, feeling appreciated can go a long way, especially with someone who is committed, passionate, and dedicated to the work like me. I didn't then and still don't work for public accolades. But given the fact that I didn't receive any promotion in this particular position, not even a title change, at least there could have been the public acknowledgement of my accomplishments. I honestly didn't think that this was a difficult task since I had seen it happen for other team members and close colleagues. This is when it is important to be grounded in your personal vision and mission, so that you can stay focused.

How you handle tough times and difficult situations can make or break your future moves. While you may feel that things could be different, you must continue to work, and the work should continue to be done with the utmost integrity. I have seen people struggle with this for years. People have a hard time maintaining integrity during times of distress, and when there is mistreatment, a hostile work environment, compensation or role confusion, matters can be far more challenging. For me, during these tough times, I really relied on my relationship with God. And for those of you reading this book, you too will have to pull from some higher power as a source of strength. This was vital for me because I needed this strength daily, especially since I was expected to perform well under pressure – all while feeling under-valued. Reading the word of God and other positive words helped me tremendously. Whether at my desk or in a meeting, I would read scriptures that I put in my journal. I remember being in a meeting where I was having a courageous but yet challenging discussion. Throughout the meeting, I periodically read the scriptures, and they calmed me and helped me to be rational and hopeful.

One day while sitting at my desk, I recalled all of these events and wondered how things were going to be the following year. Considering the state of affairs at work and my current performance, which produced positive outcomes and made the company look good, I asked myself: *What is going to happen if I perform like this next year or even better?* Now this became the million-dollar question for me. The answer was not readily available and the crickets in my mind grew bigger by the minute. As you might imagine, I wasn't too hopeful. Then these words pierced my thinking: *If you perform well, the likelihood of something positive happening is low.* I paused for a few seconds and asked myself, "*Why*"? And the answer was this: *Nothing will happen because you are now only competing with yourself.* This had to be one of the biggest aha moments that I have ever had. Not because it was a strategy for increase or a promotion. It was an aha moment because it gave me much needed closure. Sometimes you will find that in your journey to grow and increase financially, closure provides the space you need to make moves and take immediate next steps. Needless to say, after this thought-provoking moment, I got a new job in less than 120 days.

While I didn't have the fairy-tale ending with a promotion and increase or that corner office, I did get clarity and the information needed to make the best, most informed decision for myself. This decision to move on shifted my trajectory for the better. I was presented with a new opportunity that allowed me to get in the door at a high-level, which added value to my professional portfolio. The position didn't come with a significant pay increase, but it did come with an increased portfolio of work that later benefited me in many different ways. This work came with more visibility, political support, and more public interfacing.

Getting in the door is not as simple as it may sound. Things won't just fall from the sky once you get in the door. It requires hard work on your part. You have to be intentional about working in a way that shows you have a greater capacity than where you are. When I first started in the foot-in-the-door position, I was intentional about working hard and going the extra mile to prove that I was worth a promotion and upgrade. The key is not getting discouraged when you don't see immediate results. You have to keep pushing until an opportunity comes that is a great fit for you and will give the compensation that you desire. Building relationships helped me as well. As I mentioned, the temp assignment I was given put me before key stakeholders, who eventually gave the green light for my promotion. When you get a foot-in-the-door job, then you must work hard and perform all the duties associated with the position even if they are extremely easy. As a business owner, if you offer free services and products, you must do that expecting there will be no payment or that you may have to discount something. However, you just never know. You may get some kind of compensation. The point is that you should operate as if you will not. Don't lose focus because you are consumed by climbing the ladder. You must remember the job that you are getting paid to do. Your diligence and attention to the work at hand will more than likely be impressive to managers.

That's why, it is essential to exhibit good work habits that can set you apart from your peers like dependability, being a self-starter, integrity, timeliness and consistency. Even if you are over-qualified for the job, you still have to perform. This concept is important. If this opportunity is going to get you in the door, then you need to perform. This is not the time to say things like "I am not getting paid for this" or "I am over-qualified." Continue to remember your "end in mind," which is getting in the door as well as increasing your salary level to six figures.

These attributes will set you up for success. Even if an organization doesn't have a position for you, with these qualities they will look for one and make a way. A potential client will find the money and pay you for your services and goods. There are certain qualities that employers look for when they decide to promote someone. Always remember that no matter what type of job you have or get, you are just getting your feet in the door. Managers always look for people who appear to be hard workers. They are also willing to take a risk and hire you because they know you are a hard worker. If your integrity is not questionable, this helps them feel that they can trust you should they decide to promote you. If you have you own business, you have to consider the above as well because it will determine whether you will get that client or will they move on unimpressed with you.

"There are certain qualities employees look for that can accelerate you to your next level!"

You need a plan so that you are clear about what you want and need to do. It is important to develop a strategy for getting your feet in the door. This is like anything else you do in life; you need a plan. Your plan steers you in the right direction. It is OK to think about it, but it is important to put it in writing so that you will have a visual reference. The plan you create becomes the blueprint that drives all of your decisions. It will eventually become your map for success. Getting your feet in the door just might be the easy part. Executing and sticking to your plan could be tough and challenging. There are moments where you may have to tweak the plan, but what helps is that a plan exists. I'm sure that those who have experienced any level of success will tell you that they had some kind of plan. The desire to get a degree, a business or a good paying job is usually the thing that motivates the development of the plan. One of the practices that I love in the business arena is the demand for a business plan before you start.

The business world understands the necessity of having a business plan because that plan sets the tone for your business. It's simple. We all learned about maps in school and how to read them. We were taught to read them so that we could get directions as needed. A map tells you how to get from point A to point B. The plan that you create for your personal development will help you migrate from one experience to the next until you reach your final destination, which is that dream job, business or venture. As you proceed and grow in life, your career or your business, it is so important to always keep your desires and what you want to do at the forefront of your thinking. Being clear and sound about what you want to do will give you the confidence needed along the journey as you make critical decisions that are connected to your goals. Having a plan that is aligned with your goals will help sustain your momentum, even when times get rough. You may have a job that you don't like or you may be in a field that is not aligned with what you want to do or with the ultimate goal you have set. My advice to you is to continue to look forward and see the end in mind. You may ask, "What is the end?" The end in mind is the thing that you long for, the thing that causes you to go to school or to write the business plan. I'm not going to mislead you into thinking that knowing what you want and having a plan are the magical things that you hold onto without stress or strain then all of a sudden everything you ever wanted unfolds perfectly. But, what I am saying is, having an end in mind will give you a better appreciation for where you started and where you want to end up. What I will say is that your plan will keep you going and strengthened when you get discouraged.

There will be moments when you may question yourself, even if you have selected the best career, industry or business. This is when you have to be confident in what you know you want and your plan for your career or business. You may begin to seek out that promotion and don't get any offers but it does not mean that you will never get a promotion. Most of the time it's all about timing and positioning. During these times, persistence is what will be the thing that will move on your behalf. You can't give up because you would essentially be giving up on yourself. If you give up on yourself, how can you expect for others to stick with you. If you don't believe in yourself, who will? Just because someone tells you no, it doesn't mean that you are doing the wrong thing or selected a bad career or business. It simply means that you must move forward. No one has that confidence in what you should be doing but you. This essentially means that no matter what happens, who says no or thinks you are not qualified, you must continue to push. Push for what, you may ask? Push for your end in mind, that ultimate goal and place you want to be. It means you must embrace yourself with your own confidence. Let self-confidence be your friend when you feel like you want to give up. You have to know that you bring value.

Whether it is to an organization or school or with the products and services you offer. Whenever I am faced with getting a lot of "no's" and trust me, I know this oh so well. I have consistently reminded myself of what I am worth and that I add value. Things didn't come for me easy and my trajectory at times has felt like a steep hill that I was climbing. Many days, I got winded, tired, and discouraged, and wanted to cry. Many days, you will feel the same. You may want to cry; if so, do that. Crying is like being on that steep hill and all of a sudden you fall. You may scratch your knee in the fall, do that. But just like that hill, you stand tall. Pick yourself up after you cry and continue to push. There are so many successful people who can share this same sentiment. Many of them wanted to give up when they were told "no," but they didn't. They had the ability to pull from within to keep going. And this is what you are going to have to do as well.

"No's should be viewed as a nice opportunity and not rejection."

You have to be persistent even when you hear "no." This can be very challenging for some people. Viewing a "no" as a nice opportunity instead of rejection will give you longevity. Why does a "no" have to be viewed as rejection? The primary reason is that we take it personally. You have to remember to keep all things in perspective. Early in my professional career as I began in the business world, I was consumed by the "no's." I was an emotional wreck. I thought something was wrong with me. Essentially, we equate "no" with something is wrong with us. Hearing "no" does not have to put you in a negative space if you keep things in perspective. My husband always poses this question when people are having difficult times or struggles: "Is your glass half empty or half full?" When I first heard this question and really thought about the significance of it, my life changed for the better. My husband's question challenged me to think differently and reconsider my perspective.

The thrust of this question is perception. My husband believes that life is all about your perception. He doesn't want you to forget about your current circumstance, which is the reality. However, he does want you to focus on your outlook. He forces you to strongly think about how you view your situation. What does a particular situation look like from your lens? Essentially, we can control how things are viewed. You can see your glass as half empty or half full. I'm sure you agree having a glass that is half full is better on any day than having a glass that is half empty.

People should see tenacity, determination, drive, flexibility, commitment and persistence when they see you. Potential employees or clients should say he or she will not stop sending me their resume, press kit, proposal or curriculum vitae. Don't cave in to the negative aspects of the process. The negative thoughts can begin to steer you in the wrong direction. Embrace these times, but don't let it consume you. These rough moments are not always bad; those times help to build your professional character and give you a greater appreciation for what you are trying to obtain.

So when you finally get that promotion or that ideal client, you know how to handle it because you worked so hard to get it, and you don't want to mistreat it or lose it. You won't mistreat the elevation because you know it didn't come easy for you. I consistently remind myself that people don't have to extend opportunities to you or take risks in patronizing your business. You will have to be grateful for all of the experiences you are afforded with. Gratitude will go a long way. In fact, gratitude is a key to success and helps to sustain you. During tough times, I reminded myself that things would get better and that one day I would be doing exactly what I wanted to do. The key to being authentically grateful during difficulties is finding something that you can be grateful for. It may be having flexibility on the job or a nice work schedule. You do what I call "make it work for you." Take that something and build on it for strength and fortitude. I remember during this time my boss didn't make a big fuss when I had to leave early to pick up my kids from school. That was a big deal for me. So even though I wanted more from the position and deserved it, I was grateful for the flexibility so that I could pick up my kids every day. This eliminated the need for me to pay close to $1,000 a week for after-school care for three children.

Gratitude is going to keep you and it will help you to be patient. In the end, it is all worth it. Knowing what you want to do, that ultimate goal, will guide you through the good and bad times in a poised manner. You will one day look back and see everything that you learned through the process. Take all of the growing pains and use them as lessons learned for the next job, opportunity or business deal.

You should remain civilized through it all, even when you want to throw in the towel. Remember, how you respond to "no" determines how you ultimately embrace your "yes." Your response does matter. Don't be so focused on the negative aspect of the "no" that you miss being grateful when you get the "yes." Don't get that one great opportunity and then complain about every little thing, thus messing up the moment. In order to survive tough times, you are going to also need lots of patience. That patience is going to give you the stamina that you need.

You have to be willing to do whatever it takes to accomplish your goals and to materialize your dreams. If you are working in an area that is not aligned with your goals, then you may want to consider volunteering in the area that you want to be in. Requesting to do a special project in another department could be an option for you. Joining a task force or committee could add value as well. The only thing that I suggest is that you are honest and upfront with your supervisor so that you don't come off as being disloyal. It is not a bad thing to participate in a project related to your field that is in another office. Just make sure your manager is clear. If you are not comfortable, figure out a way to be transparent. It is important that you share your goals with your manager if you are comfortable, so that he or she is also clear and could possibly assist you. For those in business, you can connect with a business owner who specializes in a particular body of work that you are interested in. The person could potentially serve as your coach or mentor you as you work to get experience.

Knowing it's time to realign is important when you are working towards a six figure plus income. I decided to realign my goals when I discovered that I was working for an organization that had great opportunities but those opportunities were not aligned with my career goals. I requested to meet with my immediate supervisor and shared my concerns around my current work not being aligned with my goals. I noted that I had been generous and gracious in the process, and once I decided to start looking for another job, I began an aggressive job search. This was my authentic attempt to be transparent. During my search I identified prevalent weaknesses that I needed to work on so that I could advance. I also identified new skills that I had to develop immediately.

Having the ability to discern when you need to acquire new skills for advancement is paramount. The skills you had when you started your career or business may not be the same skills you need to sustain you and that will get you the financial increases that you desire. This is from a longevity and sustainability perspective. It is essential to stay abreast of current trends and best practices in your

71

area of expertise or business. Make sure you zero in on the things that really matter when it's time for you to go to another level or to get a promotion. We can spin our wheels for decades working hard, staying in the office late, neglecting our families, and this could get you nowhere. You can get whatever you need; skills, support, coaching, etc., without neglecting your family and yourself.

We typically neglect ourselves and go above and beyond because it can lend itself to acknowledgement, increase and rewards by superiors and the general public. With all of this, you can still be behind in business and career trends that will ultimately increase your capacity. In order to avoid this, you must establish your goals. This will help you with time management and prioritizing. Once you prioritize, you have to work your plan and stick with it to accomplish those goals. People will make you feel like you have to go above and beyond to work. That is all fine and well, however you must work smarter and not harder. Get a pulse on the skills and duties that you need to help you get promotions with six-figure salaries or an overflow of clients. This will be what will take you above and beyond what you could have ever imagined. There are some sacrifices involved, but you can have balance. Neglect and isolation is not going to guarantee that you will be elevated, receive a promotion or get that great contract. You certainly will have late nights and early mornings, but it has to all be in perspective. I personally learned this the hard way. Almost had divorce papers to show for it.

Two years into my marriage, my job was my most prized priority. It's not that I didn't love my husband and family dearly, but I thought I was doing the right thing professionally – climbing the company ladder. I had to quickly change my work norms so that I could save my marriage. It wasn't easy at first because I felt like I was going to miss some opportunities if I was not considered to be a hard worker. It wasn't until I worked hard with no reward or promotion that I understood that the personal sacrifice wasn't really worth it. I don't want to say that you shouldn't work hard because it is needed. You just need to keep things balanced for yourself. I got sick one year after working really hard and not taking care of my health, and I didn't receive any award for overdoing it. You can imagine how I felt. I had lost precious time with my family, time focusing on my own professional capacity and the return didn't match. Let's shift gears just a little.

Knowing when you are ready to transition to six figures is paramount. There are three key areas that drive decisions for you to enter into the six-figure arena. The areas are **data**, **budget capacity**, and **human capital management**. These are typical areas that you need to have some experience in unless you have some amazing product or some type of invention. Make sure you have a reference point and experience in these areas. No one will consider compensating you with a six-figure salary if you haven't ever managed at that level. From a management perspective, you want to make sure you have these skills in your portfolio. When you matriculate to the six figure income bracket, people are paying you to make the best decisions for their organization based on your level of expertise. Of course, there are always exceptions. How can you lead a team of 10, 20 or 30 if you never supervised a staff? This type of question is one you may have to ask yourself as you work to increase your earning potential. As your income is increasing so should your savings.

This is why I can't stress enough the importance of why financial planning is critical. At every level you should be saving money so that you can fund those big dreams and goals. You want to do that even if you are stuck in a job or have only a few clients. Saving every pay period is the best way to start. Having a savings can help you support your exit strategy if you are working a full-time job. When you are in business, your savings will keep your business going. It is essential that you consult and work with a financial coach. One who will be able to guide you with all of your financial planning needs including investing.

Finding the right stocks and bonds are important. My husband was instrumental in making sure I was investing and saving.

This paid off when I didn't get a raise for many years in a row. Some of the basic investing tips include buying stock in companies that you routinely patronize. You may be in a situation where you feel like you can't save because you are not making much. You can't afford not to save. If you scrutinize your money and what you bring in, you will see that you have more room to save than you think. It may not be as much as your colleagues, but at least you are saving. As a business owner and professional, you want to save for a rainy day. This puts you in the financial position to be able to cover unexpected expenses. You may get an opportunity that requires you to cover upfront costs and fees. If you don't save, living only pay check to pay check, gig to gig, then you might have to forfeit an opportunity because of your financial situation. It is important to ensure that your finances are solid and in- tact.

When you are sound financially, then you can help those in need and pay it forward. It's important to note that I never aspired to gain a six figure income so that I could just be the only one to benefit. I wanted to be a blessing to many. Giving to charity is also important regarding positioning yourself and in general. It is always good to just be in a position where you can give to worthy causes. We all started somewhere and sometimes your donations go further than what you think. Not to mention, opportunities that could benefit you professionally or personally may come from an organization that you are giving to. It is not always about donating money. You could also donate services, goods and time. When I think about giving, these two quotes pretty much sum it up:

*"No one has ever become poor by giving." — **Anne Frank, Diary of Anne Frank: The Play***

"It's not how much we give but how much love we put into giving." — ***Mother Teresa***

SIX STEPS TO SIX FIGURES
Planner

What are your next steps?

_____

_____

_____

List any barriers

_____

_____

_____

What resources do you need?

_____

_____

_____

Completion Date

_____

_____

_____

Reflections

_____

_____

_____

_____

_____

_____

_____

_____

_____

_____

_____

_____

_____

_____

_____

_____

_____

_____

_____

_____

Reflections

_____

_____

_____

_____

_____

_____

_____

_____

_____

_____

_____

_____

_____

_____

_____

_____

_____

_____

_____

_____

Reflections

_____

_____

_____

_____

_____

_____

_____

_____

_____

_____

_____

_____

_____

_____

_____

_____

_____

_____

_____

_____

_____

Step 3

HARD WORK PAYS OFF

DON'T TAKE NO FOR AN ANSWER

If someone tells you "no" then, you have asked the wrong person. In life, you will discover that rewards and benefits won't always come in the form of money, contracts, cars or awards. There will be times when you may by choice or force take on various tasks, assignments, and projects that may not compensate immediately but bring a great reward at the end. You may have been in this kind of situation and thought, what are the benefits? Over time, you may have wondered where was the additional compensation for all of these extra assignments and tasks? And if you are like me, you don't want to hear the spill about "other duties as assigned". There was a time during my career track when I had to take on extra projects without compensation. I carried a workload that felt like it should have been split between two to three people. I did all of this and did not receive one extra penny.

At one point during my tenure with a particular employer, I was promoted but didn't get a pay increase; I didn't even get an upgrade in parking. All I could say was "wow." I remember the moment like it was yesterday. My boss told me that he wanted me to be a director of a new office. My heart pounded with excitement. Finally, my hard work was paying off! And that was all I could think about. I immediately started planning for the work of the new position. As time went on, I became acclimated to the new position. I noticed though that my salary did not increase. I remember thinking: I am sure it is just some type of a delay because I know I am getting a salary increase for this new position. This new position came with new work and a new title. During this time, I was also working as a Realtor but was only doing it on a part-time basis. I really did not leverage my real estate business at the time, and this was another lesson learned. Never put all of your eggs in one basket. So one day I asked my boss about the salary and was told that the new position did not come with a raise. When I asked why, my boss said it was just a lateral move with only a title change.

This was devastating for me because I was feeling overworked and underpaid. Not being considered for a salary increase was inconceivable. Remember, I was executing two jobs, and all of this made me feel demoralized professionally. This didn't settle well with me also because I knew of my counterparts in similar situations who received salary increases. This was a struggle until one day I decided to make the situation work for me. I was tired of crying and feeling bad for myself. I began to think of ways that I could benefit from what I thought was the worst time in my career. During stressful times like these, you have to be able to process the negative emotions when you encounter discouraging situations. Keep your "why" before you. At this point, I also started being more intentional about expanding my other businesses.

When it sunk in that I was not going to receive the financial compensation that I deserved, I started scrutinizing every aspect of my job, including projects, tasks, deliverables, and events. I did this so that I could determine what would add value to my resume and help me ascertain the job of my dreams along with the salary that I desired. Believing that something good would come from my situation gave me the motivation I needed to remain in it until a better opportunity came along. This experience shifted my entire perspective. I so needed this because I felt like I was in a losing battle. I had to walk in faith in order to push forward. This plan of action eventually paid off when I finally landed a job that yielded close to a $10,000 salary increase. I was able to get this new job because of the experiences that I acquired during the time when I was not getting recognized or compensated. It was at this moment that I began to really feel like my hard work was paying off. I thought about the many jobs that I had applied for and did not get an interview. It seemed like rejection was never going to get old. I had to embrace the disappointments and stand on the shoulders of my pain until there was a brighter day. I came to realize that God was not going to waste my pain. I knew that all of this was not about me not being qualified. I was more than qualified, yet it still hurt. I remember the feeling every time a potential employer would call me or email me. I would be excited, and then I would hear that they were not planning to move forward with me. This feeling was quite overwhelming at times. I would feel so discouraged. It was a lot for me considering the amount of resumes I had sent out and was only contacted by two or three employers.

Getting the new job was a mental release for me because not only did I receive an increase in my salary, but I was starting during the heart of the recession. This was such a relief because I had been searching for a job for well over one year. I had been on a serious and consistent employment hunt and was not getting any calls, and very few interviews were scheduled. Over a one-year time and after sending my resume to over 100 employers, I only received three return calls and two interviews. None of those employers hired me. I was really close to being hired for one job, which I was excited about because it was a vice president position. I advanced through the interview process and became a finalist, but after much deliberation the employer decided to hire another candidate because they didn't feel that I had the exact skillset needed to effectively thrive. It turns out that the skills I didn't have for the position were the same skills I later acquired by managing the two roles that I didn't get compensation for. I had planned lots of events and managed projects. These skills ended up helping me execute my first big project on one of my new jobs. It was a training summit for over 100 people where I was responsible for the overall planning and facilitation.

All of the above applies to entrepreneurs as well. You have to find ways to build your customer/client base. Try offering free services or if that does not work, you could consider discounting your fees as a way to attract customers. I did this when I launched my second business, a fashion company. I started fashion consulting because I always loved fashion and shopping. The business provided image consulting, styling, personal shopping, and freelance fashion design services.

In the beginning, I styled many people for free as a way to promote my business and services to the general public. It was like free marketing. Who would turn down free marketing? This is a great motivating question to ask when you are just starting out and your finances are not where you would like them to be. This was a great way for me to generate a buzz while perfecting my craft. During the early stages of your business, you may need to perfect your craft and offer free services to help you do just that.

So the time came when I resigned from my previous position so that I could start the new job. This was a great day for me but slightly bittersweet. It was great because I felt like I was finally getting what I deserved. It was bittersweet because there was a small part of me that wanted things to work out with my old employer. I wanted to feel validated by them, and the additional compensation would have done that for me. I should not have given any employer that kind of power over my dreams. I quickly learned a valuable lesson that continues to help me to this day. This situation forced me to understand the importance of self-value and confidence. I was looking for organizations and managers to validate me, but ultimately I owned that power.

When I started the new job, I carried this philosophy about taking on extra projects and assignments that do not come with additional compensation. I did whatever my manager asked me to do even if it was a task that was not part of my job description. Remember I told you about the job I was detailed too? What I forgot to tell you was at first, I thought I was being reassigned for doing something wrong. I asked my co-worker, who was detailed with me, if she was aware of something that I had done wrong, which could explain the detail. My co-worker noted that we were not detailed because we had done something wrong, but rather because we were good workers who had produced for the organization. This time, I was not expecting additional compensation based on my past experience. While I know there are HR protections for job-related matters like details and additional assignments, I was not getting my hopes up for extra pay. Because I am a hard worker by nature, I dived right in at the new office. I began to see how this detail could accelerate me in the organization if I played my cards right, worked hard and was effective.

Two months into the detail, three top director positions became available. These positions were part of my division and connected to an expansion initiative that my new boss was leading. While working the detail assignment, I still reported to my current manager, who was one of two managers I had before the detail. I supported both managers and they shared supervision over me. Initially, I was concerned about the shared management. I had never experienced that before. However, it wasn't as bad as I thought it would be. I exhibited respect for each of them, and because I had a good rapport with both managers, I was able to pursue one of the available director positions. When I reviewed the job descriptions, I was happy to see that I met all of the qualifying factors. After consulting with my husband, I decided to submit my resume and application. Seeking wise counsel is critical when making quick moves professionally and in business. You want to make sure that you are operating at a high level of understanding and integrity.

It is also important to remember that when you make a transition, such as going to a new office, people are watching you in the new location. You want people to know that you are dependable and committed to the work and not focused on jumping on every opportunity that is presented. You want them to know that you are stable. This was a critical point for me because I had just started this new job and things were happening fast. I certainly didn't want my supervisors to question my integrity. I was willing to forgo applying for a director position if it meant that my boss felt like I was not committed to the work directly connected to my division. Integrity matters and is important as you progress professionally and in business. What I've often observed is those without integrity typically don't last long. To be clear, integrity is defined by Webster as: The quality of being honest and having strong moral principles, moral uprightness. Integrity is not throwing people "under the bus" for your own personal gain or skewing the truth.

Another key to success as you pave the way in your career or business is mentorship. Getting a mentor will not only help you in your craft, but it can ease some of the growing pains that you may experience. I have personally benefited from mentorship and coaching. I can't imagine what my career and business trajectory would be like without mentorship. I have benefited by gleaning from those in my fields and have learned so much. I eventually started a mentorship business that involved group classes and one-on-one coaching. Before starting my fashion business in 2006, I spent a lot of time studying and researching all the aspects of the industry. This extensive research helped me tremendously and I was able to adjust and modify my business plan based on my research. Market research is critical when starting a business. It is also helpful when you are considering a new career. You just can't jump out there and launch a business or start a career without some critical demographic information. You should know the need, the competition and anything else that is out there. With all of the information that is publicly available, you should be well informed about your industries landscape.

Launching my second business was like embarking on a second career. I assumed that the transition would be easy, but boy, was this far from the truth. I was in for a rude awakening. This process was a challenging one partially because I didn't have an extensive background in the fashion arena, and I didn't know a lot of people in the industry. Without a lot of experience, I had to build a network of colleagues as well as a solid client base. Although I faced roadblocks, I believed I would get past all potential barriers. I was confident in my ability and potential to grow. At times, it was discouraging and I felt like I was in insolation. It didn't seem like I had any help. Those that I attempted to connect with were not willing to partner and share.

One day it hit me: I need a mentor. I needed someone in the industry who could develop me and show me the ropes along the way. So I decided to consult a friend who was in the fashion industry. I was skeptical initially because I thought she would not want to share her expertise like others who I had approached and were not willing to help me. I took a leap of faith and asked my friend to mentor me, and she said yes. I was excited because I definitely needed coaching. I needed help with figuring out how to juggle a full-time job and a couple of part-time business ventures. There's definitely an art in balancing a career and business.

Be careful when selecting a mentor because you want to make sure that you're being guided in the right direction. Don't mistakenly choose a mentor based on solely outward appearance or personality. Mentorship is not about personality; it is about connecting with that right person who can build your capacity. Your mentor should have more knowledge and experience than you. They should have documented results in a particular field. I recall my first interaction with my friend when she was serving as my mentor. She allowed me to work on a project with her and that experience was so rewarding and refreshing. I was so moved by this gesture that all the "no's" I had previously gotten faded away. After much determination in getting my business started, I was excited about having a mentor. I was exciting about the possibilities that were presented. I was excited about increasing my capacity. This one opportunity gave me the momentum I needed to move forward. Sometimes all it takes is one good opportunity to make up the difference for all of the bad opportunities.

In your walk of life, you are bound to encounter "no" at some point or another. It is inevitable. "No" doesn't mean that it will never happen, it just means that you may have to wait things out. I want to encourage every entrepreneur and professional to make it a point to give back. Take some time to help someone who is just getting in a particular field or someone who just needs a mentor to push them and drive them to their next level.

Overall, I must say that this was the best experience that I could have ever received. My friend/mentor allowed me to get my feet wet by giving me different assignments related to my field. While I was working on different things, I watched her and took plenty of mental notes. I couldn't stop thanking her because I was grateful. This process taught me a lot, but more importantly I understood the power of having support. There were so many things I learned through mentorship, and I will never forget them. Having a mentor was invaluable and I could never repay my friend/mentor. There are times throughout your career and your journey as an entrepreneur when things will not work out as planned. But you can't let it get you down. If you fall when you are rejected, then you get back up and search for your acceptance. Throughout my career, I heard "no" a lot and I mean a lot. There were times when I would beat myself up if I was turned down for a job, business contract, or promotion. I realized that every opportunity I pursued was not necessarily what I should have been doing at the time.

Don't let anything cause you to lose your momentum. Keep exploring opportunities and keep pushing. Exploring options is not as bad as others think. This exploration allows you to stay connected with current trends in your field. It also keeps you positive about your capacity and what you can do. You will also have time to assess what areas you need to strengthen. The same applies when you are trying to get business and contracts from potential clients. You could submit a proposal, and it could be turned down. You could encounter customers who don't want the services or goods you have to offer. But know you can't give up because what's in front of you is greater than your present circumstance.

SIX STEPS TO SIX FIGURES
Planner

What are your next steps?

_____

_____

_____

List any barriers

_____

_____

_____

What resources do you need?

_____

_____

_____

Completion Date

_____

_____

_____

WOW!!!
WORDS OF WISDOM

Success

Success is not measured and defined by how much money you make, your title, the car you drive or the clothes you wear. Success is measured and defined by the positive impact you have had in the lives of people. Who are you changing?

Reflections

_____
_____
_____
_____
_____
_____
_____
_____
_____
_____
_____
_____
_____
_____
_____
_____
_____
_____
_____

Reflections

_____

_____

_____

_____

_____

_____

_____

_____

_____

_____

_____

_____

_____

_____

_____

_____

_____

_____

_____

_____

Reflections

Reflections

_____

_____

_____

_____

_____

_____

_____

_____

_____

_____

_____

_____

_____

_____

_____

_____

_____

Step 4

DON'T BE AFRAID TO TAKE RISKS

PREPARATION & PLANNING ARE KEY

Taking risks is like stepping out of your bed onto the floor. As your feet proceed to land on the carpet, ceramic tile or hardwood floors, you take for granted that something is there. In all actuality, you could be stepping on nails, glass, metal, rocks, wood chips, or no floor at all. What makes us feel so assured that you are stepping down on the floor even without looking is "confidence." How can you have this kind of undisturbed confidence when stepping on the floor from your bed but not in other areas of your life? I know that this analogy could appear low level in nature but it is the harsh reality for so many. You must embrace this same type of confidence in all affairs of your life. If you are going to really become successful and maintain that success, you are going to have to take risks. Taking risks is essential for all professionals and entrepreneurs. Confidence will motivate you and give you the courage that you need to take risks. Risk taking creates a win-win scenario for you. It becomes a win-win for you because even if you fail, you learn from the failure. But winning puts you one step closer to your goal. In order for you to fully engage in risk-taking behaviors, you have to be courageous and confident. The main reason why many people are afraid to take risks – and I was in that category – is because of the fear of failure. The thought of potentially failing at something has been a debilitating barrier for so many people. But, failure is part of life. You will experience failure more than once throughout your life. It's one of the main ingredients for success. If you poll most successful people, I'm sure many will tell you one or two things:

They failed at something at least one time.

They took risks here and there.

Most people are afraid to take risks because they know failure is a possible option. When we take risks, we have to also be responsible for the outcome. But the outcome could be success, so in that regard, it's worth the risk. Failure could be the result of taking a risk but not in all cases. It's just a possibility. On the other hand, your success could be on the other side of that possibility. When you don't take risks, you run the chance of not knocking on the door of success.

"Confidence will give you the courage that you need to take risks"

My question to you: Why would you run away from knocking on the door of possible success? Suppose success answers, and you are able to walk through that door. We run away from success because we know that failure lurks close by. Are you really willing to forfeit the successes of life because you are afraid to take a risk? What is the worst thing that could happen? They say no and you have to start over again. I'm not suggesting that you make irrational decisions because taking risks requires seriously thinking things through and doing what's best for your current situation. This is critical so that you are clear about what you are doing.

You have to know the appropriate timing for risk taking. If you only have one income, then that may not be the time to decide to leave your job to start your business. It's all about timing. Proper timing helps to create the most beneficial situation for you. Taking risks is like flipping a coin – success is on one side, and failure is on the other. Again, learn from your failures. Sometimes you are put in tight situations for a purpose/reason. I can recall feeling so bad because I was applying for so many jobs. These are jobs that I know I was more than qualified for. One day I decided to have a conversation with my manager about my overdue compensation. It had been caught up in Human Resources cycle for over one year. During that talk, I questioned some things and advocated for myself. I walked out that meeting feeling so empowered because I stood up for myself. In that one meeting I found my voice.

We wake up every day with certain assurances and con-stants. By this, I'm referring to things that we expect to happen like waking up, brushing your teeth, drinking, and eating. Typically, these things you don't have to plan for daily because they are just part of our routine. However, there are some things in our lives that don't automatically happen on a daily basis. There are things that you must plan for and require a level of intentionality. Your future is one that requires much planning and preparation. One of the rea-sons why goal setting is so important is because it allows you to prepare and be thoughtful about what you want to do. Planning and preparation are critical elements for taking risks.

Anything you aspire to do will require you to plan and pre-pare for it. It does not matter if you want to be a dancer, basketball player, teacher, preacher, banker, singer or a freelance photogra-pher, you must plan for it. What are you planning for? You are plan-ning so that you will have the necessary actions and steps needed to be successful. So how do you get started? Do you need formal education, in the form of a college degree? Can I do this without having a job on the side or other gigs? All of these are questions one would ask at this critical stage of planning.

It's the planning that gives you the ability to take risks be-cause you are clear about what you need and what you have to do.

Most people don't like to take risks because they are unclear or un-
sure about what they want to do or they feel more comfortable
being in a situation that appears to be safe. Preparation and planning
gives you the tools that you need to take risks. If you make a bad
decision as a result of risk taking, your plan can easily get you back
on track. Taking risks and not having a plan can be a dangerous
combination and a recipe for disaster. You will not know what direction to go in after the risk. The plan and risk has to be paired.

Please understand how important planning is needed if you are
going to get on the road to six figures. If you want success and six
figures, then planning and preparation are the key ingredients for
your success. Planning means that you are thoughtful and intentional about what you want. Preparation ensures that you are always ready and you have the capacity to handle whatever comes
your way. Essentially, you know what you should be doing. Your
plan should ultimately align with the established goals you set for
yourself.

Having a vision and putting that vision on paper aids in the
planning and preparation process. There is power in writing your
vision. Your vision is simply what you ultimately want to be and
achieve. If you desire to be a world renowned speaker, then this becomes your vision, your ultimate goal for yourself. Write it as a
statement when putting it on paper. A vision that is captured on

paper serves as a visual reminder and can be a motivator during difficult and challenging times. Your vision is what drives all of your long-term and short-term goals. Goals should accompany any vision because they support and give you clarity about what you should be doing. Goals help keep things in perspective as you reflect on what you have done and still need to do. They also allow you to track progress or the lack therefore. I can recall pondering on many things I wanted do and accomplish. There were so many creative ideas that filled my mind on a given day. What I ended up realizing was these ideas stayed in my mind and never made it to paper. I assumed that I had the capacity to keep everything in my head and pull it out when the time was appropriate. This didn't become a harsh reality until one day I found myself trying to remember the details of something big that I wanted to accomplish. I did everything I could do to try to bring back the details, but unfortunately, nothing worked. As a result of not capturing my vision on paper, I subsequently lost it. What a travesty! This was a great idea that could have generated lots of revenue for me. How devastating was this!

Instantly my life changed drastically after I realized I had lost what was potentially a lucrative idea. I was determined to make the best out of this situation and decided to start writing down things from that day forward. Journals, pens, notebooks and paper became my best friends. I immediately purchased a journal just for my ideas and vision. I wrote everything in that journal, every single detail. Shortly after this, I saw things change slowly for the better. What I learned thru my new adapted practice was when you write your ideas and vision down, you add value to it. You make it important the minute you take time to scribe it. The mere fact that you thought enough of your vision to write it means that it can materialize. What you don't write down you typically don't value.

As a business owner, putting your vision in writing is essential. This document is called a business plan. A business plan is a tool used to ensure that there is a clear roadmap. Your business plan is usually put in place before your business launches. It is not advisable to start a business without having everything mapped out in writing. If you start a business without a business plan, you run the risk of failing and making lots of mistakes. Part of your business plan should include the financial aspects of the business. The financial portion of your plan helps you sort your financial needs and the capacity of your company. You must ensure the financial integrity of your business is outlined in the plan. When you write these things down, you can hold yourself accountable. You have to have a strategy that includes the basic business essentials. You must know the strategy that will help you maintain financial stability as an entrepreneur, and those who have a career. This is not just for everyday people that desire a piece of the American dream/pie. Understanding your financial capacity will guide you as you make important business and career decisions.

Let's talk a little about tracking your spending. Tracking spending will help you identify any financial gaps and give you a clear indication as to whether or not you are moving in the right direction. I was one that always engaged in frivolous spending until my husband took my credit cards away from me. I was only able to make purchases if I had cash. Although very painful, I learned a lot that helped me along the way. It made me think about my spending differently. This also was a wake-up call, and it forced me to scrutinize every purchase since I had a limited cash flow. Once my money was gone, that was it until it was time for me to get more. Things changed when I decided to track my spending. I was spending beyond my means. This is one sure way to get you in debt and to stay there. I didn't create a fancy spreadsheet; I just used my notepad on my mobile phone and starting listing every expense with dates and amounts. It was easy to see where I was wasting money and what legitimate purchases I had made. My husband had me on a serious spending plan.

If I started out with $500, then I would write down all of my purchases with the dates so that I could see how much and how fast I was spending after receiving my "allowance." By doing this

I discovered that one of my problems was buying a lot of coffee, which was depleting my funds. I so loved coffee and couldn't imagine having to cut back. The tracker showed me how my miscellaneous expenses were caught up in my overall spending. The key to tracking your spending is capturing every expense, whether big or small. You must be honest about what you are spending and the frequency.

SIX STEPS TO SIX FIGURES
Planner

What are your next steps?

_____

_____

_____

List any barriers

_____

_____

_____

What resources do you need?

_____

_____

_____

Completion Date

_____

_____

_____

WOW!!!
WORDS OF WISDOM

Invest in Yourself

You are worth it. Take some time to read a book, magazine or just go to the spa. You may even want to get a self-help book that aligns with a dream or vision you have. If you don't invest in yourself, who will? Remember, you are worth it.

Reflections

_____

_____

_____

_____

_____

_____

_____

_____

_____

_____

_____

_____

_____

_____

_____

_____

_____

_____

_____

Reflections

Reflections

Step 5

THE POWER OF STARTING OVER

*USING A PORTFOLIO TO MARKET YOUR
STRENGTHS FOR A FRESH START*

Starting over is not always a bad thing. It is important to have a plan so that if you have to start over, you know what route to take. While it could be a very difficult time, regrouping is not always negative. Carefully evaluate the situation so that you can capture all learning opportunities. This is especially critical if you are starting over because of a bad decision, inabilities or deficiencies. You must find out the cause and rectify any problems so that you can move forward for ultimate success. It is important to assess your fiscal capacity and stamina because you will have to make decisions swiftly to maintain yourself and/or your family. Having a savings is a great safety net when starting over. This money can support your transition until you find a new job, and re-establish your client base. If you don't have extra money, you will need a plan for sustaining while re-establishing yourself.

"Starting over can give you a fresh wind that is needed to catapult into something new."

It's always good to know what's out in the market, even when you are in a good place. This gives you the upper hand and allows you to make quick connections. One way to have the upper hand in this type of situation is to have a current resume, press kit, and/or portfolio. This will allow you to quickly seek out available opportunities. Be in the habit of knowing what jobs are on the market as well as which potential clients may need your services. This means even when things are going well, you should still be searching for opportunities just in case you need a Plan B. There's nothing wrong with staying abreast of what is out there. No matter what job I had, I always searched the industry to see what opportunities were out there. Checking out the market gives you further insight on what employers and potential contracts seek out.

Starting over can also give you the fresh wind that is needed to catapult into something new. It's easy to get comfortable in a job, business venture or other type of effort. The hardest part of all of it is exploring different things and being willing to move out of the comfort zones. For those who are comfortable in your current state, starting over may be just what you need. This gives you an opportunity to focus on you and to see what is happening in different industries. You also put yourself in a position to be seen by those who would not have otherwise seen you. Your season of starting over could be the very thing that produces an opportunity of a lifetime. You could be making room for your big moment.

Once you have determined that starting over is something that must happen, the next step is ensuring that you have a way to document all of your experiences. One way to document your experiences is by using a portfolio. A portfolio is a collection of work that highlights your skills and abilities. It is important for you to showcase what you really can do. It sets you apart from the people who say they can do, but don't have the proof. For those in business, you want to showcase your work by way of a press kit. This collection of work samples can be displayed in different ways. The most common way to display your collection is paper-based. The work is organized in a three-ring binder notebook with dividers for each section. Another way to showcase your handiwork is via an electronic portfolio, which may include videos, audio or photography. You can create the portfolio as a slideshow presentation. Visuals capture people's attention. They give you what you need to seal the deal.

Remember that your brand is still your brand even when starting over. It is going to be up to you to make sure that your personal brand is not tarnished. One way to do this is to make sure the public knows that you still produce good work and that your business still provides quality services and goods. There was a time in my career when I decided to leave my good job as a school administrator because I wanted to start my own educational consulting business. Needless to say, I left that job and I left without a plan. I am not sure what I was thinking. Maybe I thought clients were just going to fall out of the sky. I even pulled funds out my retirement account. I was using this as my start-up capital. What a horrible idea this was. Less than a month after I left my job, my grandmother got sick, and I had to exhaust the money that I had pulled from my retirement to supplement her insurance and her other needs.

Within a year, the consulting business was not thriving. I had only one or two clients. By the end of the first year, I was broke, in financial distress and had to go back into the workforce. This all felt like an epic failure. Here I was a businesswoman without a plan who left a stable job. What I later came to understand was the issue wasn't me leaving my job. The issue was leaving without a plan. I really had egg splattered on my face because I had to go back to working for someone and had to do it quickly. I had no more money left. The only option I had was to go back to the classroom as a teacher. The painful part of this transition was that I had to take a pay cut of $30,000. The salary of a teacher was far less than the salary of an administrator; just in case you didn't know. Yikes! This was a hard pill to swallow, but it was something I had to do. I had to deal with the embarrassment that I felt. I worried about what people were thinking about me because here I was back in a school, not as an administrator but a teacher. I gave myself a few days for a pity party and then decided that I was going to go in that classroom and be a rock star because my brand was on the line. I did just that, I worked hard and I got special recognition for my work over a three-year period. I was even featured in the local newspaper! I promised myself that I would keep the consulting business going and leverage it on a part-time basis as an additional income stream.

This experience showed me that I had the capacity to push past some intense pain and disappointment. I was only able to do this after I recognized my fault in the matter. Once that happened, I forged ahead. You have to be honest with yourself first before you can move on from this type of set-back. This is not the time to blame others, it is the time to look from within. For me, starting over was one of the best experiences in my life. I ultimately recognized that starting over doesn't always have to be a negative thing. You can learn from your mistakes and grow from them. You can maintain your integrity and work ethic through the process and yield some positive results.

SIX FIGURE ROAD BLOCK
Lack of Credentials

SIX STEPS TO SIX FIGURES
Planner

What are your next steps?

_____

_____

_____

List any barriers

_____

_____

_____

What resources do you need?

_____

_____

_____

Completion Date

_____

_____

_____

SIX FIGURE ROAD BLOCK
Lack of Confidence

Reflections

_____
_____
_____
_____
_____
_____
_____
_____
_____
_____
_____
_____
_____
_____
_____
_____
_____
_____
_____

Reflections

Reflections

_____
_____
_____
_____
_____
_____
_____
_____
_____
_____
_____
_____
_____
_____
_____
_____
_____
_____
_____
_____

Reflections

_____

_____

_____

_____

_____

_____

_____

_____

_____

_____

_____

_____

_____

_____

_____

_____

_____

_____

_____

_____

_____

Step 6

KNOW WHEN YOU ARE IN DEMAND

MAINTAINING SIX FIGURES/CELEBRATE SUCCESS

As you progress throughout your career or as an entrepreneur know that it is essential to capture in a professional way your work and your endorsers. Document what you have to offer and your track record. This essentially puts your qualifiers out on the table. Having those whom you have worked for and provided services for speak on your behalf or write positive testimonies is important. This helps you understand when you are in demand. Each person's road to success is different, and therefore identifying pivotal moments of your career and business journey are important. This can help you gauge whether or not you are in demand. When someone is making strong and passionate requests for you, you are in demand. If suddenly you get several requests for your expertise from potential employers or clients wanting a special good or service, you are in demand.

Being in demand means that the public at large seeks you out for what you have to offer. Being in demand denotes that what you have to offer is wanted by many around you. It means there is something about your work that people gravitate to such as good customer service and the quality of your work. When you begin to get consistent multiple requests for what you have to offer or sell, this is a good sign that you are in demand. Once you are in demand, you can also impose demands to create an advantageous scenario for you and your business. This is the time when you can aggressively negotiate salaries, fees and service delivery expectations. When many people want or need what you offer, you can easily raise rates or secure additional work to bring in more income. This will definitely put you on an accelerated track to making six figures. Oftentimes, you become a person in demand because people like what you do and how you do it. Maybe you can identify a significant solution to a problem or provide instant results when people work with you. Essentially your brand is tight, and you have a solid track record of keeping your promise to the public. This is huge because it doesn't matter how great you are with your business or career, if you don't keep your promise to the public, you will not be in demand. People may speak negative things about you, and this could ultimately damage your personal and business brands.

Developing a desired niche could create a demand for you. Building a successful niche is not about popularity, rather it is about your ability to respond to and meet the needs of the public. I remember getting requests from several organizations to help with early childhood program development. Initially, I didn't understand why because this area was what I called one of my outlier services from my company. What I later realized was that I had created a niche for my business. If you create a niche area with quality products or services, you will eventually be in demand. I remember one particular job where the employer refused to pay me more money. Although they didn't want to pay me, they continued to ask me to stay because no one in the organization knew the work like I did. I had created a niche for myself without even knowing it. Equipping yourself will allow you to be in the position of high demand. Here is that word "planning" again. It is so critical and you will not experience sustained results without it. Being in demand requires planning like anything else. You have to plan for what is next. Determine if you have the capacity, the bandwidth, and resources to meet the demand. Can you fulfill the multiple requests coming in? Do you have enough product? Do you have adequate promotional materials? Becoming someone in demand takes time but once you are in demand you will need a plan for staying in demand.

Part of the planning process could involve identifying if you should go to college or trade school to get the appropriate skills, credentials or degrees. If certain opportunities require a level of education, and you don't have it then you can't expect to be in demand for those moments. This is important because qualifications do matter. Be clear about what you need, so that you can get everything that will best position you to be in demand. The preparation is essential and will ensure that you are properly equipped to handle the many requests ahead.

There was a time when I was up for a position and a salary increase was discussed. I was told later that I could not receive that increase because I didn't have a master's degree. This was some of the most devastating news I had ever heard. Here I was working extremely hard and producing results, but yet I could not be rewarded for it because I didn't have the right combination of skills. People will not request to use you, hire you or promote you without the necessary skills. Producing good results will attract people to you, but not necessarily create a demand for you, especially if you don't have all of the qualifications.

After you have established a strong track record, you can then celebrate and acknowledge all of your hard work and accomplishments. Celebrating success keeps you motivated and gives you the stamina needed when things get rough or when things slow down. One ritual to consider when celebrating is capturing small milestones incrementally. Both big and small accomplishments should be celebrated. Know that the small things matter and you should not overlook them because they are not big in your eyes. It does not matter how you start but what matters the most is how you finish. You should not feel ashamed of the small endeavors because those will be the ones that push you into the big moments.

Again, managing your finances is a must if you plan to shift to or maintain a six figure income. You just don't want to make six figures, but you want to maintain it. You have to have a plan for your finances so that it can serve as a strong foundation to support you. This financial support is instrumental when going through difficult times. As you begin to get salary increases and multiple contracts, think about where your money is going. Don't get caught up in material things like cars, clothes, and fine dining. Those things are great, but you shouldn't let them cause you to lose sight of the importance of maintaining your six figures. One way to maintain a six figure plus income is to have multiple streams of income. Most rich and successful people will tell you that they have multiple streams of income. I have always had a minimum of three streams of income. Now I am up to seven different streams. Multiple streams will help you when one slows down, you'll have others moving. You have to be very strategic when managing multiple streams of income. Each stream should get your attention on a regular basis. You don't want to jump in multiple areas, just because it may seem popular. You want to jump into different areas, because you truly want to increase your earnings.

Once your finances start to flow, you need to make sure you keep what you have. This involves intense money management. If you are not savvy in the area of financial management, then consider seeking a financial expert. I had to do that and it was the best thing I ever did. I had to get my personal financial affairs together before I was able to get my business affairs together. My husband specialized in money management, and he was my lifesaver. He helped me save, invest and grow my money. One quick way to save your money is to shop more from the sales rack. Many people pay regular price for nice things. I purchase most of my items from the sales rack. I save a lot of money when I do that. You must make time to scrutinize all finances you have coming in and going out. I was able to start my third business with my own money because of the financial lessons I had learned over the years. You have to know when to capitalize on your financial gains and success. You can't spend every bonus or contract you get. You should even leverage certain projects that you work on. You may not get compensated for them at the moment, but another job could pay you more for doing the same thing.

Having a savings account that you don't touch will also aid in keeping your finances intact. Again, I was not good with money management personally, and I knew that it was going to be bad for my business if I did not learn to save and invest my money. Investing is important. You have to have a plan for growing your money if you want to maintain six figures. The growth plan will cause you to create a financial cushion for yourself and will give you the capacity to fund your visions. If you operate like "money grows on trees" then you will sink financially quicker than you can float. My worst financial experience was when I was a real estate investor. I purchased a property and sold it after three years. This was my first investment property. There were no issues with selling this property because it was in a highly desirable neighborhood.

It was a great purchase, and I knew that it was going to increase me financially when I purchased it. During this time, I was also a teacher promoted to an administrator. I had two other businesses, including educational consulting. I also got my real estate license to sell homes. I was working these multiple streams of income to my benefit, which allowed me to get my first luxury car.

When I sold the home, the proceeds I received was very close to $300,000. This was a major milestone for me. Coming from humble beginnings and receiving assistance from the government, this made me so proud and happy. Who would have thought that a single mother who was a teen mom would ever see this kind of money before the age of 30? This was a true testimony. Once I received the money, I paid some bills and bought lots of material things. The mistake I made was not having a plan in place, and subsequently, I spent that entire 300k money in less than 12 months. This was a hard lesson for me. I submitted to the financial teachings from my husband, and I embraced better financial practices. Years later I got back to six figures. The journey back to my six figure income was difficult and painful. I literally had to start from ground zero. I planned, pre-pared, set goals and focused on implementation. It was hard though for me to imagine that I would ever make six figures again. I prom-ised myself that I would work hard until I achieved it. And I did just that. But this time I not only saw six figures again, I maintained it.

SIX STEPS TO SIX FIGURES
Planner

What are your next steps?

_____

_____

_____

List any barriers

_____

_____

_____

What resources do you need?

_____

_____

_____

Completion Date

_____

_____

_____

Reflections

_____

_____

_____

_____

_____

_____

_____

_____

_____

_____

_____

_____

_____

_____

_____

_____

_____

_____

Reflections

Reflections

Reflections

_____

_____

_____

_____

_____

_____

_____

_____

_____

_____

_____

_____

_____

_____

_____

_____

_____

_____

_____

_____

SIX STEP TO SIX FIGURES

MINI TOOLKIT
6 ESSENTIAL RESOURCES
TO GET YOU CLOSER TO
SIX FIGURES

GOALS

List your top 5 goals that you would like to accomplish within the next 60-90 days.

Key words to consider when developing goals:
Realistic & Measurable

1._____

2._____

3._____

4._____

5._____

HOW MUCH DO YOU WANT TO MAKE?

Write amount inside of box.

BIG ROCKS

List every rock that you must move in order to get closer to Six Figures

1._____

2._____

3._____

4._____

5._____

6._____

7._____

8._____

9._____

10._____

VISION STATEMENT
(Personal)

VISION STATEMENT
(Business)

VISION STATEMENT
(Career)

LONG-TERM PLANNING

What will your business or career look like?

In 2 years

_____

_____

_____

In 3 years

_____

_____

_____

In 5 years

_____

_____

_____

_____

Connect with Rochelle Wilson on Social Media
(FaceBook, Twitter or Instagram)
@EllehcorBoutique

Rochelle Wilson is a Certified Professional Trainer in
Education, Transformational Speaker, Expert Consultant,
Lecturer and Career/Business Coach. For more
information on booking requests, email us at
SuccessGeeks@gmail.com or visit our website at
www.successgeeks.com.